World Community

(2015)

*

a research essay

*

Traumear

*

*

In order to be able to escape from the modern conditioning, which would have us assume that modernity or some development of it is feasible as a final state of mature human life, we must have a notion of somewhere better to which we might escape. The journey to what I call world-community passes through our inward, liberated human nature before it discovers world-being. Just as modernity has for two millennia been the refusal to countenance achieved human-natural liberty as an established fact, so can we now understand world community as arising out of an acceptance of that liberty, and this allows us in turn to evolve, ultimately to have eternal life in world that is mystery and sacrament.

*

World Community

It is a simple enough thing to imagine all the peoples of the world getting along together in peace and harmony. Neither does it stress us overly to think how in that case that would be the end of crisis and catastrophe, since in various predictable ways we do bring misfortune on ourselves.

What takes us closer to the brink of the imponderable is the unavoidable feeling that every step in that direction has to begin from within ourselves. It is I and not you who has to take that first step – and every step thereafter. The wish to be able to depend on politicians and governments has to be laid aside; since politicians represent us, so in a sense they are ourselves over again, while governments finally only exist to limit our excesses. Modern governments even take it upon themselves to stimulate us out of our indolence.

We take the first step towards world community

when we take advantage of the fact that we can think for ourselves. We may wish to do this among those who think what they have been told to think. We may also decide to do it when grief, sorrow and pain threaten to overwhelm us. Thirdly we may find ourselves doing it when we are persecuted for our love of god and what we are most likely to think then may well surprise us because it will strike us as utterly new.

Whenever we think for ourselves, taking advantage of the fact that we can, the world, or some part of it will appear to us in a new light and very likely we will realize we have been wrong about something, have made mistakes in the past we might have avoided or failed to take advantage of good opportunities that came our way. Emotion such as guilt, regret and remorse may well limit our freedom for a while and the reason for this is that we will pay attention and learn. Such emotion is not to stop us from thinking what we are thinking but rather to persuade us to think things out in order to clear our mind. What we think out then is what persuaded us to think for ourselves in the beginning.

*

A vision – the vision – of the peoples of the world living in harmony is given to those who have what it takes to bring that reality a little closer. We might call it creative vision, and it encompasses all that is and all beings, though first and foremost human beings.

Perhaps we should make an effort to define what we mean by *world*. It will help us to imagine it as something we are part of – but equally as something we may be in without being part of it. In other words it is not necessary for us to be involved in the fabric of the world even though we quite readily might admit that we live in it.

We know that we live in the world because we harbour certain images of it, such as a place, an institution, a system of laws and liberties, and so on. We believe we are born into the world, in other words into various given situations and relationships and an as adults we may like to think of ourselves as men or women of the world, who are worldly-wise or perhaps world-weary. "The world is too much with us" a poet laments, and mentions "getting and spending" and alienation from "nature" as causes of the malaise. One philosopher speaks of the world as "will and representation" while another says that it is "all that is the case" and goes on from there for many pages. Many children are taught that 'god made the world' and some may know what to make of that. Is the world everything? they ask. What of nature? What of the *earth*? Oh, the world is round, we all know that. Silly people used to think it was flat.

2

So is the world the earth? Some have spoken of the possibility of a plurality of worlds and if that were indeed found to be the case, I would have to specify my own world in comparison to yours. Some Christians believe that Christ came into the world and left it again, returning to them in his kingdom within them.

Is it indeed possible that every one of us has his own point of view and opinion of the world and of what constitutes it, so that a great part of many of our tasks will be precisely a coming to terms with one another over what each of us means by world before we build an edifice of mutual understanding? Exactly how feasible is that, one wonders. Are we members of a worldly, secular society or do we also have spiritual aims and sources of communality? Does the temporal and the other-worldly, spiritual dimension come together for us in our world or are we forever torn between the two, hankering for both and at home in neither? As Christians we believe that Christ saved the world, making it unnecessary for us to be weighed down by uncertainty and guilt while we exist so that we may do our creative work and live rather than die. As infidels, as heathens or pagans, we want nothing to do with this generous gesture of God called Christ and we try our best to get along without it. The hermit in his hermitage presumably has 'turned away from the world', as has the monk in his cell. The world here really means the affairs and even the presence of people, of men, women and children and their various joys and cares. Certainly when we go to a quiet little room to pray or meditate, we may be described as having, for the duration, left the world outside the door. Or perhaps we take time to remove from our soul the 'cares of the world'.

People at times amuse themselves 'at the expense of the world', when they behave as though there were no such thing while they enjoy a movie or march to war. In both cases the popular mind is abstracted and might not uncharitably be described as other-worldly.

3

Then of course there is a great to-do in many places about the beginning of the world. We people cannot help ourselves, we must speculate about the beginning and end of things. Genesis stories abound and so do end-of-the-world apocalypses. The need to turn even the world into a thing is embedded in our questionable nature. We question it and it questions us. An unavoidable excitement about matter as such stimulates a curiosity even about the origin of the universes. If a thing exists it must have started somewhere and we want to know when, presumably so that we can start one ourselves. Those who are gifted with the ability to bear up under the contemplation of beings, prior to their protectively veiled existence as things, demonstrate a beguiling willingness to let them be and to delight in them as they do that. All that is appeals to us and sets us innumerable quintessential examples. As people we are content to pass by. Horseman, pass by. We cast a cold eye on life, on death, to quote from the famous epitaph. As human beings we take pleasure in the fact that we are, we delight in our existential prerogatives, we sing and dance for no reason whatsoever except to celebrate spontaneously.

Let's change the world, we say, not necessarily for the better but a change is as good as a rest. Of course we must persuade those who might be willing to help us that it will be an improvement of sorts, so we show ourselves endlessly clever and inventive. We instigate revolutions, even in other countries. We manipulate their power structures to bring about 'regime change'. And why not? We cannot allow the world to stagnate. War and peace are psychic correctives. We have broken our mirrors but that was only a start.

Finally, surely, it comes down to how the world influences and affects us and how we in turn react and respond. Such is the perception of world as condition, situation, surroundings and environment. We interact and correspond. Only by being part of the world can we have prestige in it. The man of the world looks to how others perceive him. He deals in appearances. He does not ask what is right but what might come next. Acclaim and opprobrium define his thought processes, alter his mental climate.

Whom shall we set next to the man of the world? Surely the man of god. The world, like so much else, is in his gift and he knows it. Less concerned with beginnings and ends, aware of the difference between myth and reality, he prefers to speak of world rather than of the world because this allows him to come to terms much better with his various obligations and responsibilities as a learner and as someone with power and skills.

How could a man of god and a man of the world converse? Would they be able to agree on a common language? Let's try it. They sit next to each other on an airplane:

M.G.: Good morning. You have the aisle seat and you have the longer legs. First flight to Moldova?

M.W.: No. fourth time. You?

M.G.: First time. Meeting the wife in Chisinau. Concert pianist. I try to catch up with her now and again.

M.W.: Pianist eh? Does that pay nowadays?

M.G.: Not at her level yet. It will if she manages to make a name for herself.

M.W.: Always the same, eh. If you cannot get bums into seats you're a lost cause. What about yourself? In business?

M.G.: No, I'm not smart enough for that. What about you?

M.W.: I work for the CIS. Commonwealth of Independent States. Moldova is Europe-centred. Looking for membership in the Union.

M.G.: Any chance? What do you suppose?

M.W.: Oh, very likely. It's all about money, isn't it.

M.G.: I suppose so. Sad, isn't it. Not much community spirit if it's all about money.

M.W.: Economic Interdependence. What else is there? We all lean on everyone else. Like a big crap game. You learn how to guess smart what the other fellow is holding. My duties are mostly in the line of diplomacy. I say yes or no depending on what the other fellow wants to hear. So what's your work?

M.G.: I'm working right now.

M.W.: How's that?

M.G.: I listen to you. I hear what you're saying. I make ready to respond in a useful way.

M.W.: You don't say. What would be useful in that case?

M.G.: You sound jaded. Bored with your life. Maybe with life in general. – Ah, finally! We're moving.

M.W.: And so?

M.G.: So I try to inject a bit of joy into your soul.

M.W.: That's embarrassing. I dare say you know that. All the same, thanks for the good intention but I don't consider I have a soul. That is old-fashioned, isn't it?

M.G.: Depends how you look at it. For me it's like a built-in gyro. Let's me know when I'm speeding, loitering, generally straying off the path. You must have something like that, surely.

M.W.: Yes, I see. Like when I'm feeling good about something or somebody. That's my soul, is it? That feeling?

M.G.: Not really a feeling, no. More like a sense of awareness of being around and glad of it. I notice it most when I exercise my good will. When I intend advantage for the fellow next to me.

M.W.: Like me right now?

M.G.: Exactly.

M.W.: Can't say I follow you. I think you're kidding yourself. Sounds like pie in the sky, idealistic nonsense, no offence. I don't prescribe to any religion. Can't afford that in my business. Have to treat everybody equal. You're welcome to your views, of course. I go to church, for policy's sake. Better for me if I'm known as a church-going person. I don't believe in God. Too much cruelty in the hearts of believers. No siree. God won't look to me for support. There's these fellows cutting off heads to please their God. Count me out. I'm in complete favour of a secular society. It's hard graft but you've got to eat. I have to support two daughters in a fancy school. It's the wife's choice, not mine. Should make her earn the money for it, ha. Fat chance. Oh, it's not as bad as I make it sound. My health is still pretty good and I carry weight in a few committees. I don't know why I'm talking so much. I usually don't, to strangers.

M.G.: You're a sincere man. I enjoy talking to you – and listening. Besides it shortens the flight, doesn't it.

M.W.: Well, thank you for that. I'm sorry now, I didn't mean to insult you. You just think different, that's all. If we had met in some official capacity I would have been wearing a mask and I would have had stock-of-the-trade phrases ready on hand. You must have got under my skin.

M.G.: Or under the mask you weren't wearing.

*

So it seems, from our little experiment, that the man of the world and the man of god can get on. This is splendid news, especially since we do not equate the man of god with a religious man. Surely religion as such, not different religions, cut across any divide we might come up with when studying man-

7

kind. In fact mankind and religion are inseparable. Those who nowadays say they want nothing to do with religion merely wish to distance themselves from superstition, from abuses of power and from fanaticism and the like, and for this we cannot blame them. As soon as they meet a thoroughly religious man, who perhaps adheres to no particular religion, it is as if they cannot help but honour him because they sense their own underlying religious nature.

And what is a *religious nature*? Or rather ask: In what way is nature itself religious, whether human or otherwise? It is religious in that it strains towards communion. All that is born and grows is natural. All that comes into being, develops and evolves demonstrates an affinity with all else.

Our knowledge of man is that we see his religious striving not only from without, as we see all other beings and things, but also from within, we ourselves being men. When this is forgotten we tend to make the presumptuous mistake of imagining religion as outward observance and so we feel the inward dimension as a separate need, a longing in vain for satisfaction.

As men, as members of the human species, we are able to take the responsibility for both our inward and our outward dimension. When we neglect one or the other we become stunted and we stultify.

So we can say that our very nature is religious in that it tends to a proper and clear separation of the outward and the inward realm followed by a union. Both go on at the same time, at different rates, and differently in each one of us. This is natural. It is what goes on whether we like it or not. We can declare war on it if we like and turn into freaks of one sort or another. We can point to freaks in every department of the world: Freaks scientific, religious, ethical, social, personal etc. We can also ignore it, take no account of it, remain indifferent to it, be contemptuous of it – and become nonentities, stumbling-blocks to our fellow man. Both the freak and the nonentity are extreme concepts of course. They are the Scylla and Charybdis between which active men and women, who value the knowledge and understanding of their religious nature, conduct themselves; as they behave, do, act and create.

What we mean by revealed religion, in comparison to natural religion, is the result of our knowledge and understanding of natural religion. So we question our religious nature, preferably in a spirit of meekness and humility, and what is, as a result and in its own good time, revealed to us is both the son of man and the son of god. Inwardly the son of god is revealed to us and outwardly the son of man. This is what is revealed to us and we manage to discern a clear distinction between our inward and outward being – and even as we know full well that in reality we are one.

Now as we pass from the dream of childhood to the rationality of adulthood we distinguish clearly and, if required, educationally, more clearly between the world without us and our thought and feeling within and we learn that through work and good deed, plus increasing awareness, we may bring those two, the within and the without, together more and more perfectly, so that we imagine how it must be a great satisfaction for us if perfection were actually achieved. The desire for such perfection fires us. Some advance to the point of the son of god within and the son of man without, which sets off a truly dramatic and productive tension within them. We would be silly not to take advantage of those in the past who have worked to 'bridge' the identified gap between the within and the without, let us say between the world and the soul. When now we hear of someone who has done this in terms of the son of man and the son of god, we experience an unmistakable excitement. Greater love than this is unimaginable. When we now discover how the achievements of this person have in fact made possible the achievements of many others whose guidance we have ap-

9

preciated, in personal presence, in books, in music etc. we are exceedingly grateful and must call those fools indeed who deplore that someone has indeed even allowed himself to be murdered for the truth and now they cannot be the first. (I make reference to a phenomenon that draws our attention at the present day!)

With surpassing joy we realize we have all we need to achieve perfection. We become truly creative. Our works, whether little, large or great (surpassing) flow from us with ease. Our conduct becomes unquestionable. Our behaviour is no longer critical but informed by love. We do what we do with good will and sound intellect. We act because we have something worthwhile to contribute.

So it appears that the man of the world and the man of god, mythic creatures as they both are, need not avoid each other, for the gap between them has been bridged.

*

In a community, people think for themselves. The same goes for world community. The people who select politicians – let us call them caretakers – to look after the general business of the country, think for themselves. As a direct consequence those they select think for themselves. They make up their own minds, listen intelligently to the expressed thought of others, are possibly influenced by it and take responsibility for subsequent conclusions. All people in a community rule their own affairs, either directly or through selected care-takers.

If I am not ready to behave in a communal way – if I have not yet arrived at that level of maturity, or perhaps I have, through neglect, become immature, then the members of my community will see this not as a punishable offence but more like a temporary shortcoming or amendable misfortune.

An outright unwillingness to behave communally testifies to a choice to behave socially, and it is from our comparison of community with society that we have much to gain.

For a start, community members know and recognize one another. These are, among much else, religious people who are not necessarily members of any particular religion. Community cuts across all religions.

Society, on the other hand, is something different. Something like a contract is involved, as we know also from the numerous studies of that topic during the past two hundred years. Societies are bounded, each by some individual point of view that defines their sodality. The belonging or not belonging to a society depends on outwardly identifiable criteria. Clubs, fraternities, guilds and unions are all social in that same sense. A passport, a card, a number or name allows for identification. Companionship, at best, not compassion is what counts, whereas for community to work, *empathy* and *compassion* are indispensable. The struggle and frequent disparity between individual liberty and State control that has to be faced by every society if a temporary stability is to succeed has no bearing on communal living or on the community spirit.

Community spirit makes sense, social spirit does not.

To serve us in our study of universal or world community, the difference between society and community is more to the point than that between societies and communities. The most appropriate description of society is therefore that of a preparation for community. Also what interests much more than world community as an ideal or utopia – which actually does not interest us at all – is progress towards world community as reality, in which case society and sociability certainly would only get in our way if we chose to think of it as an end in itself rather than as part of the approach to world community.

11

As social individuals we need to be urged away from ideal-ist or utopian thinking. As communal people we see no diffi-culty in behaving in world-communal ways. A telling charac-teristic of world community is always that the talk cannot sepa-rate from the walk. Someone is able to preach the excellent tenets of John Stuart Mill with some limited persuasion even though he lives and behaves disreputably. Communal living is at once more difficult but also simpler. Once compassion is mastered and becomes more than a fleeting emotion, communi-ty is a simple and straightforward matter of just getting on with it. Compassionate thinking and feeling, and behaviour and ac-tion, go hand in hand, because conscience is taken for granted. The difficulty comes in whenever our intelligent compassion is challenged. Of course this is unavoidable, because we grow. Only in an ideal state, in a utopia, is growth dispensed with – and along with it all practicality. It never makes sense to com-pare myth with reality.

Every challenge to our mature compassion is bound to throw our thinking and feeling into a degree of disarray. We learn to identify these episodes of disarray. We welcome them as harbingers of greater maturity, of compassion more finely attuned to actuality, in short, of more power, which is power to do good and the only power a communal being can honestly acknowledge.

*

If we want to avoid catastrophe, interest should really be taken in the transition from social to communal thinking and behaving. The onus cannot but be on those who are themselves capable of communal thought. They are the ones who know the difference. Beyond that, they will thrive as members of world community to the extent that they put themselves out for those who are unhappy with society and perhaps show an interest in universal or world community. The communal spirit does not rest in itself but it reaches out. We might say that outreach is part and parcel of its character. As such, of course, it competes with many other spirits, who seek to draw individuals away from social reasonability, towards irresponsible liberty or ideological enslavement. The communal spirit does not persuade except by example.

The catastrophe we avoid by espousing communal spirit causes us to tremble when we think upon it. It amounts to the dissociation of our members. While we seek society as an end in itself we prevent communal spirit, and this is more serious than remaining ignorant of it. However, as we are discovering in our own time, it is the immature who are ignorant of communal spirit who most readily fall into the clutches of those who preach the social spirit as an end in itself. It turns out to be a terrifying end in itself. Eventually after much peripheral damage done, it collapses.

The modern Christian spirit is commonly nothing more than an attempt to prolong society-in-itself by means of Judeo-religious morality. Consequently the struggle seems never-ending. A comic arrogance rises to the surfaces when these Judeo-Christians, who perhaps have a notion of world-communal spirit but will not personally act upon it to bring it into reality, presume to be able to destroy the very spirit of destruction incorporated by those who aim at the perfect society.

History shows us that whenever a people becomes too self-absorbed in society as an end in itself, a merciful reminder brings this to their attention and stops them in their tracks. Equally we do well to keep in mind that religion is not enough to keep us out of the clutches of the supra-societal spirit when it once again steps onto the world stage to remind all and sundry of just that fact. Religion, as our love of god and of our fellow man next to us, itself requires completion, but in combination with the social spirit alone, that is to say in the absence of

13

communal spirit, it turns into show and sentimentality. This sentimentality is much more of a fault than the superstitiousness with which religions so often are charged, while the show, the splendour, the aesthetic charisma, displace the glory and renown of god – of the god who especially loves children.

*

People cannot cope without religion but religion requires completion. Even those who reject this or that religion cannot cope without religion. What I mean when I say they cannot cope is that they cannot succeed in what is the first and foremost desirable requirement of every human being, namely the recognition of humanity and human nature within. Irreligion is nothing more (or less) than dispensation with this essential requirement.

Once we recognize our humanity and human nature within, we automatically wish to acknowledge it outwardly. We sense that this can only be done truthfully. However now the problems start. How can I proclaim my humanity? How can I exemplify my human nature? Religion itself is a coming to terms with inward values by means of love. Whether we love god or the person next to us, it amounts to the same, and certainly this gets us within sight of the promised land, which should be described as the realization in space, time and causality of the truth that our religion and our religious behaviour, our loving of god and neighbour, shows us, lets us feel and sense, and above all lets us think. We yearn for this realization. Perhaps we desire it. We do not feel content if we cannot come out with the truth and the beauty, so that not man, nor our fellow man (which are abstractions), but the men, women and children of our community, have the benefit of it.

This is a tall order, of the highest calibre. Why so? On account of the many hearts and minds in our environment that adhere exclusively, or at least to an appreciable degree, to ex-

14

ternal systems and values, on which they base – or try to base – their existence.

Once we have begun to try to base our existence on external systems and values we end up having to work very hard and having to make a virtue of hard work, and also having to insist more and more that ours is the right road to travel – if only everybody would do the same. However they don't and we blame them for it. We try to persuade them to become members of our Religion, of our Political Party, of our Society and we cheer loudly when we gain the majority. We grab land, we build cathedrals, we conquer kingdoms, all in the interest of showing that our ideas and tastes and convictions are the right ones. Numbers, we suppose, will prove the point.

Those who come along now and speak of their inward knowledge – well, they fly in the face, don't they, of what we hold dear. We identify with creeds, with forms of government, with possessions – in short with the need to make survival, not to mention a particular standard of survival, the be all and end all of our life on earth – and along come these upstarts and upset our applecart. We won't let them. We will fight them tooth and nail, call them names, excommunicate them beyond the pale and generally let them know that we are right and they are wrong; even that we are good and they are bad.

I admit I am taking this to extremes. Have I not heard of the one who came right out with the facts of truth and beauty quite regardless of what those who were wedded to the outside of creation would do to him, and as if, as a consequence of his immense courage and high calling, he were not with us today, in spirit and reality, as the infallible facilitator of our truthful and beautiful journey on the earth of our choice?

I call it the earth of our choice, not because we might as readily choose Kepler-452b but so that we do not take the earth for granted but think of it, know it and enjoy it as our earth. In the last analysis of our humanity and our human nature we learn we are also caretakers of the earth on which we exist. Wedded to externals we are not caretakers but land pirates, amassers of territory, and all that is terrestrial is but grist for our opportunistic mill.

Once we have come to terms with the means by which we may round out our existence both inwardly and outwardly, in truth and beauty, we are practically bound to say yes to the earth as our earth, as our delightful responsibility.

*

Human instinct will not rest and we will not find true peace until religion comes into its own and Religions are superseded.

In order to understand this we have to realize that the purpose of religion is to bring us back into community with god. Community with god is then what explains our existence and informs our behaviour.

While we insist on being members of a Religion we close the door to that evolution of our humanity that I call god-community. Religions all tend to be final states and stages. In the same way do Nation States preclude development. International efforts and ecumenical strategies all share the same fate, which is failure.

World-community is not international. Neither it god-community ecumenical. Human instinct is the single common denominator of us all and what we learn from it – which is to say what we learn human-instinctively – allows us to plan a common future for the earth's population. Within us god-communality underpins our existence. Without us, outwardly, world community is what we build and create.

*

From the point of view of reason it should be perfectly possible to acknowledge human instinct as central to our final evolutionary changes and settlements. No longer does it make sense to perceive instinct as animal. We have come to know our animal companions much better during these recent years and we tend to the more realistic persuasion that we may sensibly speak of animal intelligence and human intelligence, of animal perception and human perception. Then finally we also allow for human instinct and animal instinct, so that our community is based around being and beings and not limited to things.

*

Instinctively then we tire of nothing so soon as of predicted events. As soon as we know something is going to happen we lose interest and take another look in the pitch darkness or in the blinding light. I limit myself to instinct here. What may be predicted, based on one sort of evidence or another, or indeed on mere signs, satisfies the intellect perhaps, but instinctively we right away arrive at the conclusion that our path does not lie in that direction. Every time we hasten to renew our familiarity with god-community within. In other words we turn inward and expect to be informed. Whatever form occurs to us now we hold up against the truth and check it for beauty.

*

We hasten to renew our familiarity with god-community within. We develop our instinct for human conversation. We concentrate on this which is truly common to all human beings and all people.

What is it that gets in the way? Ideological prejudices. Insistence on cultural practices, on religious peculiarities, on political hypocrisies. How predictably dissension and disharmony arise from every insistence on these! Of course I am religious

17

because I am a human being, but does it make me more of a human being to say the rosary, to kneel on a prayer mat, to be circumcised? This great and deplorable ignorance, that an insistence on peculiar ways and means identifies the human being, craves our attention. Muslims and Jew and Christians will not permanently communicate until they agree on religion and lay aside insistence on their Religions.

The destructive ignorance does not have to play itself out in terms of – is not limited to – this or that Religion. This or that Society with all its absolutist do's and don'ts will do just as well. Nothing can cause hatred so soon as a life-or-death stress laid on what is 'done' and what is 'not done'.

"You worship in buildings and on mountain tops," Jesus reportedly said. "We worship in reality and in the truth." This lies at the heart of what we may take to heart. Was Jesus speaking as a Christian? Of course not. Christianity came along and eventually insisted on itself as a Religion, with specific observances on which life allegedly depended. The crucial step taken by this Jesus of Nazareth, into the pitch darkness and into the blinding light, has gained advantages not for Christians but for human beings – and not in terms of external observances and practices but on the basis of inward god-communality acted out in reality, in world community.

Sensible people the world over do not shun each other but are drawn to one another – not because they attend the same mosque, the same chapel or the same synagogue but on account of their common religious humanity.

If we strive to be human rather than popular we will always behave to some extent religiously, because as we grow and overcome the heart-centred evil that hinders our coming to maturity and our persisting in mature behaviour, we will choose to fall back on love of god and fellow man. If instead we strive to be popular we will fall into savagery, brutality and Faithsanctioned egotism. We will entertain such stupidities as aiming to precipitate the hand of god by reproducing apocalyptic signs and the like. The popular man seeks to conquer the world and loses his soul. Human beings conquer themselves and gain their soul. Those who strive to be popular always gather around themselves the like-minded who willingly lay aside love of truth and appreciation of beauty.

*

Beauty is the inward glory of god and the outward manifestation of bliss and blessedness. Inwardly we know, through human natural faith and understanding, that all that truly is cannot but be peaceful and at rest, harmonious and in balance.

We are born with a tragic flaw in our soul that guarantees our success as developing and evolving human beings. Due to this flaw the 'son of man' must be raised. Children, our own children, must be raised, not left entirely to their own devices. A little schooling and training can help. Now and again some education is needful where mistakes have been made or bad habits have set in. Throughout, we as parental adults may rely on the beauty of family relationship, which itself rises and sets as peace, harmony and rest.

Now religion, wherever it deserves that name, is beautiful indeed in terms of peace, harmony and rest. There is no such thing as a religious war, but wars are often fought as strife between religions.

Peace, harmony and rest are crucial for growth in being and for the development and evolution of all beings.

I call it an evolutionary rather than a developmental change when we finally cease from insisting on merely external peculiarities and learn to appreciate, for example, inward beauty.

Now this inward beauty, like all that is good and worth-while, originates in god but requires our cooperation before we enjoy the powerful benefit from it. We do not, for comparison, merely want to fall in love and then whinge because we cannot keep falling. No, we want to learn how to love. Similarly, we want to be beautiful and not merely have moments of accidental peace, harmony and rest.

So beautiful being presupposes our acknowledgement of that tragic flaw in our soul, plus a degree of acquired understanding of it as that which reminds us of our soul once childhood gives way to puberty and then keeps us in mind of it during our adult years, painfully to the extent that we allow immaturity to take hold and gloriously while we mature and during our mature years.

So we have three elements to keep before us during this quick study of what it means to be beautiful: Firstly the tragic flaw in our soul. Secondly our yearning for peace, harmony and rest and thirdly what we can do and how we can behave to achieve inward beauty for the purpose of showing it.

Beginning with the last of those three, by inward beauty shown we do not mean being handsome, comely, pretty, good looking, that sort of thing. Those are valued by the devotees to merely external appearances, while we, who know the difference, may be charmed at times – while we have our reservations. The utmost of merely external beauty is a horror to us and endangers our peace, harmony and rest. As usual, the merely external reminds us of our insouciance (even to the point where heads begin to roll) while in itself it remains worthless.

Nothing is more human natural than to want to be beautiful. We are more powerful, more able to do good, to the degree of our beauty, always keeping in mind that to look at we may not amount to much, which is neither here nor there.

So we espouse peace, harmony and rest. Now the question has to be asked: Why do these three appeal to us? The just reason is that we need them for work and growth. Those who find work onerous and growth a nuisance would involve themselves in a terrible injustice at the same time if they tried to benefit from these roots of beauty. Corruption would engulf them, they would become incapable of mercy and therefore would not be shown mercy.

Where a sense of justice prevails however, we are free to work creatively and to grow in wisdom, which is to say peacefully. Peace is organically productive and could be called the condition of work and growth, especially if we keep in mind that for an adult, work and growth are inseparable, inasmuch as we learn and behave accordingly.

That same sense of justice allows us to appreciate the innate harmony in all being in such a way that we become harmonious within ourselves, in our thinking and feeling, and being and becoming, our acting and suffering. Justice, once again keeps us on the right track and we do well, in combination with our desire, our instinctive yearning, for god-communality, to let justice rule us as much and as often as possible, not only when we feel wronged. For the spiritually adept person justice is god's immediate effect on this personality, just as love is god's influence on him as a human being. In the interest of beauty we do well to understand justice aright. We submit to it and allow it to alter the direction of our growth, such as inquisitively, productively; and of our work, such as imperatively, casually or leisurely, etc.

Just as peace is organically productive, harmony could be said to be naturally inclusive, in that it brings us within the fold of all beings; and since all that is is substantially human, we can see how desirable for our habitation on the earth is our harmonious existence.

Rest is crucial inasmuch as it allows us to transcend borders. As we grow, say, from one insight into the next we are liable to succumb to stasis, (Religions, Nation States, Societies), to get stuck, in simpler words, and this danger, if we are fortunate, is accompanied by restlessness, so that we know we are stuck and can do something about it, such as cultivating a restful approach to what we want to achieve rather than setting out on restless world conquest. Especially by way of a restful constitution do we successfully combine work and growth, so that we neither outgrow our potential, hypertrophically (fanatical cults, extreme fundamentalism) or do our work with excessive zeal. (missionary extravagance).

These are the three strands then, identified as what is up to us in cooperation with the divine glory, to be outwardly manifested, as we grow in being through appreciation of inward beauty.

*

Our yearning for peace, harmony and rest, so that we may work and grow successfully, is satisfied to the extent that we imbibe god's justice. Divine justice 'has it in for us', we may suppose, while we insist on ourselves. Civilization, whenever it flowers, practically determines that we insist on ourselves, so it seems understandable that the civilized individual is forever bucking fate. He is never at home in himself and habitually misinterprets divine justice as instances of incomprehensible retribution. Retribution could of course be positively understood, as religious impulse, but the point here is precisely that insistence on self prevents correct understanding.

Does it seem odd to speak of divine justice as imbibed? If we think of the longing for peace (not quietude) as a thirst, it seems less far fetched. Of course if we understand right from the start that our yearning for peace, harmony and rest really implies a thirst for justice, specifically for divine justice, we would no longer be puzzled, because 'thirst for justice' is traditionally familiar to us.

*

So we may conclude that the tragic flaw in our soul, with which we are born and which comes to our attention with puberty, amounts to nothing more or less than this thirst for divine justice, which draws our attention to itself in terms of the more familiar yearning for peace, harmony and rest.

At least a degree of natural wisdom seems to be required for some before they even realize that what they are missing is peace, harmony and rest, or at least even one of these. Do we recognize a lack of peace as just that? Or do we consider right away we need some sort of medication, to mask the symptom, which may in this instance be called depression, thanks to the wisdom of the day, and the cause of it is then identified as a shortage of some chemical in the brain, which will one day be supplied artificially.

Fine. When the symptoms amass we may not be able to think straight, so we may be glad for a respite – during which then we surely do well to ascertain how the underlying and real cause of our depression is a lack of peace, is a combination of disturbed emotion and painful uncertainty, for example, whereupon we honestly yearn for peace then, which is both beneficial and profitable, especially inasmuch as it either directly or indirectly, depending on our degree of maturity, persuades us to thirst for justice and to have our thirst quenched. The depression was lack of peace, perhaps anxiety, aggravated by ignorance, by the typical materialistic prejudice that the flesh is useful.

The most common symptom which lets us know that our inward beauty is at stake is any kind of addiction, to feelings, opinions or things. We know that the purport of our inward

23

beauty is that it be shown, as the glory of god. So our addictions are like derailments of that purport, when we suppose our own glory might be shown, whereupon we are mercifully reminded of the need for divine justice, to set us straight.

When we attempt to still the legitimate thirst for divine justice by any other means, we close ourselves off for a time to the divine affect on us as persons. The onus, therefore, is on us to learn to identify as soon as possible the divine from the carnal, especially during the course of our personal behaviour. Whatever attracts us does so by means of images or directly, and divine attraction is always direct. So while we are uncertain whether we are in the presence of a divine or a carnal attraction, all we have to do is look at it directly, in which case images will dissolve. Such direct attention must of course be personal and positive and not half-hearted. Efficient poets forever show us how this is done: the dissolution of images, of carnal images, to show the divine or god.

*

It is our ability to address our human natural instinct that allows us to come up with genuine respect for all people on the earth regardless of race, morality or creed. Nothing can get in the way of that respect except someone's insistence on self, in which case we do well to suspend our judgment. This is because selfishness wipes out character and effaces personality. What is left then makes no sense to us. Not that a selfish individual is considered by us to be unworthy of respect. No, it becomes physically impossible to respect such a one. If we think of respect as an empty gesture, surely we mean something else. Knowing it as physical, as of both mind and body, implies an understanding of it as a two-way operation. The one I respect cannot remain untouched, unaffected by me, unless he insists on self, for whatever reason.

I feel obliged to ask, therefore, how the unselfish one I respect is affected by me. Does he necessarily know I respect him? Is it pleasant for him to be thus respected or is there a possibility he might be put off? Can I organize myself in such a way that the respect I show automatically has a good effect?

These are all questions I need not bother with, because by showing respect to someone I acquaint him with my inward beauty, by which he cannot but be advantageously affected. Without fear of contradiction we can say that *respect* makes a good difference.

What we cannot predict is how the one we respect will respond, if at all. The good difference may be simply absorbed by him. We in turn do not require a response. Giving evidence of our inward beauty is its own reward.

Now here is the thing that gives us pause. Should we respect those we dislike? The question arises because when we like someone we feel inclined to take him or her for granted and before we know it we no longer care. Insouciance readily accompanies inclination without our being aware of it. The result is self-regard. We suppose we communicate with someone when in fact we do not communicate at all but, you might say, we find ourselves pleasant to be with, for which there is no reward.

Hopefully we catch ourselves on and take account of our carelessness before actual selfishness sets in, in which case we would suddenly disrespect the one we initially liked. Now disrespect is always harmful, primarily for the one who disrespects and secondarily for the one we disrespect – however only if he takes it to heart.

Once we dislike someone we certainly do not feel inclined to respect him. What matters however is that we do not let inclination, for or against, dissuade us from showing respect.

25

Once we let it affect us we may also begin to wonder whether or not someone is worthy of our respect, in which case a quality judgment comes into it and we find ourselves on the wrong track altogether. After all, a selfish person is not unworthy of our respect. We simply find that, without our doing anything else, our inward beauty returns to us. So we either respect or we find ourselves walking way, without giving that individual another thought. A moment later – keep this in mind – he may stop insisting on his self and do himself some good. Those who wait until someone is worthy of their respect, which is a different kettle of fish altogether, are bound to end by assuming they are being judged harshly, perhaps when involved in some totally unrelated business.

Instinctively we turn away from the one who insists on self. No moral or ethical consideration is involved. If we notice that we tend to accuse or blame, we do well to make a point of suspending our judgment. It should not have arisen in the first place.

The time for judgment comes once we are able to respect someone. This is called right or righteous judgment, as compared to judgment for the purpose of not being judged. We are at risk of indulging in the latter once inclination turns into disrespect, as was described above. When we consider that someone is worthy or unworthy of our respect we indulge in unrighteous judgment because we fear someone may judge us and so we set out to prevent him, by getting ahead of him.

When we respect someone *we judge the common condition or situation.* Whether we like or dislike someone, respect is of the essence of our caring approach, whereupon judgment is not of a person or of an individual but of the common condition or situation, according to which we tailor our care.

It cannot be called care in reality if the common situation and condition is not sufficiently judged.

We call the condition and the situation the common one because it is of the one who cares and of the one for whom he cares. If, in some condition, I were only to care for myself, no respect would be involved; only self-respect and that is a vanity. Once we indulge in this vanity, which readily happens in public life, (stuffed shirt syndrome) where we may be more prone to the fear of being judged adversely, there it turns out then that sooner or later we are truly judged, which is not a pleasant business then, nor a comfortable one.

We judge the common condition or situation so as to understand it better. If this judgment is based on respect and not on fear, in other words if it is caring judgment, it helps us to decide exactly how to care. It may take time to arrive at such a conclusion. If I truly respect someone and intend to do him some good, it makes no sense if I mean his condition or situation and not mine, as I attempt to arrive at some decision of how to help him. I may care by speaking or by remaining silent, by praising or reproving, by interrogating or by telling a story. I may lay my hand on someone's shoulder or I may decide to step back to give him time to think.

Right judgment for the sake of good caring can turn into a good habit, so that we may find ourselves spontaneously caring appropriately at times. Such a good habit is well worth acquiring.

*

An example of adverse and not right judgment can occur when I leave my well-to-do neighbourhood and visit the poor. All I see now, perhaps, is how these people make do with very little compared with how much I need to be happy. So they must be unhappy and I decide to play the generous donor. I am judging their condition compared to mine. That is adverse judgment, which can lead to inappropriate behaviour on my part. Similarly I may visit the confines of the super-rich and my adverse judgment leads me to assume that these people must be much happier than I am and as a consequence I become envious.

Right judgment, we said, is of the common condition, so I have to wait before I judge, until I find what I have in common with those for whom I wish to care.

The wish to care is after all perfectly sensible, laudable and ethical. How to go about it effectively, that is always the burning question. Fondness, which excludes judgment of any sort, is a poor beginning and usually does more harm than good. My heart goes out to those who seem to be in pain and I set out to do their suffering for them. Mere emotion, that is to say emotions, like prejudices, are best returned to the thought processor.

By comparison, the anthropologist from a well-off background who spends years among the African Ik tribe, certainly acquires an insight of sorts into their peculiar conditions and situation, however, even though he shares their condition in a sense (for professional reasons), his intention is to study and his impulse is curiosity. He may be moved to sympathy or admiration, however his profession disallows him to care, since care would 'cloud his judgment'.

What we all have in common, which is not based on externals, on things and matters of appointment, and which allows us readily to come up with the care based on right judgment, is our human condition and situation, which we know instinctively. We do not need it pointed out ot us. Whether we see it, as a matter of fact, as care based on right judgment or right judgment based on care, it amounts to the same.

Our *human condition* then embraces both our mortality and our immortality. We are as liable to death as we are preordained to eternal life. The fact that we know this instinctively does not prevent us from turning it into an uncaring study. We do well not to go down that road. Instinct and professionalism will not share the same bed. The best way to remain instinctively alert is to allow ourselves to be inspired by the truth, which requires patience and trust.

Equally it is our common human situation that we exist on earth and in space and time. This may mean something slightly different to every individual person but if we really wish to care for others, to consolidate our humanity, we do well to take it into account to safeguard the righteousness of our judgment.

Again here what counts is instinctive knowledge of these facts. The wrong kinds of science, such as the extinct sciences, distort and draw our interest into the realm of law, where a body of knowledge is never ours.

Human instinct knows nothing of laws. It knows of the truth, of the light, of the word, of the life and of the way. These are the actual post-modern (or rather pre-modern) shapes of instinct. I use the word shape to accentuate the incomparable being of these five and draw attention to how they may be approached mythically or accepted and welcomed in reality, so that there shall be no quarrel between those who know and those who surmise, for we honour those who know and respect those who surmise.

*

Why not take a moment or two to explore these five instinctive shapes, for there is both overwhelming need and ample opportunity for us nowadays to appreciate, and perhaps even to learn to appreciate in the first place, how fortunate we are in our instinctive humanity. Soon enough we will gain assurance that reason and faith are far from being cast in the shade by what we mean by instinct and I only append the word human to show that by instinct I mean nothing of a rank lower than reason or faith. Perhaps we see little need to speak of human faith or of human reason. However it would not surprise me if in the not so distant future we would consider it useful to speak of animal instinct, animal reason and animal faith when we learn to appreciate more fully these marvellous terrestrial companions of ours.

*

1. By the <u>truth</u> then, as the first instinctive shape that interests us, we mean the beautiful fit and affinity of all that is and becomes. We need nothing else to persuade us of how we belong on earth, on familiar terms with all that exists and lives, except our timely contemplation of the truth, as we may know and experience it. However far we have strayed from ourselves as instinctively capable, the truth as shapely, like a precondition of our terrestrial happiness and blessedness, pulses within us as it awaits our recognition and awareness. How many illnesses and diseases stress and disturb us only so that our attention may be drawn to the fact that we have not yet removed ourselves from extinction and its works so that we may join in the grand celebration of our common destiny!

When we confess that something is true, do we not testify that both it and we belong to the same order of being and becoming? And if we should never know whom to thank for making it possible for us to sustain ourselves in this order of both pure and significant perfection, nonetheless we have both benefit and advantage, so that no one may disturb us by trying to chain us to some external identification. In the works of the ancients we come across extensive search for the truth and many an impulse of anticipation, along with ample consolation for not yet finding it. Even today some are misguided and pursue this ancient search as if the instinctive truth were not yet available within them.

Truthful behaviour therefore always involves our instinctive awareness of our communal environment. The concepts 'our community' and 'my community' become important, since they represent both the extent and limit of our effectiveness. Everyone behaves first of all in his or her own community, defined by power of personality and integrity of character. One cannot, nor would one wish to, step outside one's true community, because to attempt this and to presume that one does, implies a falsification of effect. We may take it for granted, happily, that any such falsification, since it militates against instinctive truth, will be brought home to us and made plain. To the extent that we pretend that our personal environment is not primarily instinctive we participate in the modern tragedy of one or more of an infinite number of possible problematic dualities. Equally is the integrity of our character marred to the extent that we step away from what we instinctively know as the truth, such as when we allow ourselves to be confused by external authorities.

Powerful (capable of doing good) personality is instinctively truthful just as integrity of character implies a reliance on instinctive truth.

Human instinctive action is truly spontaneous. We instigate change not inasmuch as we have calculated consequences but in line with what we know instinctively to be right. We readily take full responsibility for any consequences then.

*

2. The light as an instinctive shape delivers us into the realm of knowledge and understanding. As we see, so we know and what we know for a reason or purpose, to some end as it were, we understand. We rely on our human natural instinct to enlighten us.

What we mean by enlightenment may amount to a sphere of spiritual union with god or it may raise our existence to the level of genuine community. Nothing in either militates against the other.

It is the light that shapes our experience of the world and of the earth. No two of us think and feel the same. Thoughtfully and emotionally, mentally and bodily, we arrive at conclusions about what and whom we come up against and meet. If we know that the human instinctive light is ours 'to turn on', we are surely much less likely to expect satisfaction from what has to be learned, traditionally and culturally, while some part of us is 'turned off'.

What typically gets in the way of the shapely light is the accumulated darkness of our various betrayals. I call it a betrayal when I allow myself to be captivated by sensuality or self-aggrandizement. In the case of the former I spoil my accessibility to knowledge which I might otherwise have acquired through learning and in the case of the latter I close myself off to wise and loving influence. The question then is, how can such ingrained, generic darkness be dispelled? If we take no account of it, it will always act as a partial brake on our progress and growth.

An insistence, not on prolonged attempts to eradicate foolish habits but on instinctive enlightenment will do the trick. The diligence of our work habits, the exercise of our faculties, the practice of our acquired skills, the exploitation and investment of our talents, all in pursuit of world community, in cheerful and joyful pursuit, let it be said, dispels any darkness for which we are responsible. It happens to be an ongoing process. If we not only talk but also walk, we need to wash our feet. Perfection lies elsewhere.

3. The word as instinctive shape pertains to all that issues from us as expression, as talk and speech, as discussion, con-

versation and communication. Any kind of language has as its source the shapely instinctive word or it falls apart upon external analysis. We know when someone speaks to us whether he has what it takes to back it up because we find ourselves 'all ears'. Some of the so-called charismatic preachers, the televangelists, are moved by a spirit of foolishness. Those who allow themselves to be moved by that spirit, and their number is legion, become, after a time, incapable of instinctive thought and feeling and in order to exist after a fashion they tend to cling to these oracles of foolishness no matter how thoroughly their nonsense is disproved by and in the light of day.

When the Jesus of the fourth Gospel says: 'I am the truth, the light, the way' etc., he refers to his presence within us today, within us who know him and value his words, so we do well to take our time to discover this truth, this life, since it does not fall out of the sky but is resurrected within us, for example as instinctive wisdom, ready for us to relate.

4. The way refers to how we proceed in the light of day. Whatever gets in our way we refer to our instinctive powerhouse whence all our renewal activities proceed. The 'way' is the how of our behaviour, of our activity. As soon as we have decided to do some good, we may question the best way to go about it. This commences from the very moment when we hand over our know-it-all egotism to the one responsible for our growth and development. Instinctively we find our way once our instincts are cleansed. Instincts relate to personal human instinct as emotions relate to emotion or as all our ways relate to the way. First things first. Our ways and means are exercises in futility until we have set out on the way. All that is cosmic and elemental stems from our informed and reformed instinctive faculty, where the good done by others in the past is available to us – including the very best of the good. Our ability to engage with successful past deeds and true advantages within ourselves strikes us at first as not very modern and up-

to-date at all but once we lay our modernity aside, along with all our ancient and other handicaps, the way opens out for us from within. We know instinctively which step to take next. Intelligence, intellect intuition all come into their own now. Faith and reason make up their age-old quarrel too.

5. The _life_ we instinctively mean is eternal. This should not frighten us. We still have all the time in the world to live eternally. All that matters after all is that our survival values (if they really are values) spring from the eternal life rather than preventing it because we insist on them. The thousand-and-one things will always be with us. Should they, because of that, rule us?

During the search for eternal life we need to traverse the bridge from modern life to what comes afterwards. Not that eternal life is necessarily preceded by modern life. Once modernity has confused us; we need to get the stars out of our eyes. We manage this not by bending the modern life this way and that, doctoring society, choosing a better Religion or listening to scientific experts, but by searching prior to modernity, where our spirit is neither sensually attached nor spiritually contracted and therefore not afraid of desertion and the curse.

Those who want to live long will miss the boat on that score. What we do well to survive is not death, which takes care of itself, but the next hindrance, problem, handicap that appears to block us from real, eternal life, when in truth those barriers exist to persuade us in the direction of a greater abundance of life. Creatively we overcome those barriers. Creativity is the primary survival tactic inasmuch as it assigns us to life and reassigns us to more life. All creativity is therefore first and foremost instinctive and only thereafter intellectual, reasonable, etc.

Not with impunity do we disregard good willingness. Any other than good will is not to be countenanced. Both intention and insistence have to be looked at here. Certainly it makes good sense to intend to live eternally for however long we have on this earth, however it makes no good sense to insist on it because we require the tacit cooperation of the one who made it possible in the first place. With intention we may keep him in mind; however once we insist, on our rights, on our name or identity, we miss out on that cooperation and our default existence does not run true. There is a time to insist, once we are secure in our eternal life, but until then we do well to stick to good intention.

*

A typically human-instinct-inspired person – what would be his (or her) attitude to work?

First of all, he would not work because he has to work but because he wants to work. What a difference of attitude! I get up in the morning and right away I want to impress myself on the world. After all, what good is the world if I cannot interact with it? How else am I to find out who I am and what I amount to? Why was the world created – and I cannot imagine that it came about as an accident; nor did it always exist, I believe that – why was it created if not as my favourite special playground? A role has been imprinted in me and now I look for the stage where I might play it. The thrill of it starts when I am grown up, say around the age sixteen to eighteen, though some start earlier, some later. Some never grow up. We talk about them another time.

The work process might start for me when I find myself under some pressure and I decide not to blame anyone for it. That latter part is important. The world is never at fault. I try to remember that. If I am convinced that I should blame someone or something, that is not the world.

35

So I am under pressure; that is one way it starts. I hold out for a short while – without fighting back or complaining, because I have had that sort of upbringing – I notice how the pressure increases and I refer to my instinct. That is where my human talent for work resides – I have been told that and I have learned it. I was brought up to a few basics, thank goodness.

The good thing that happens now – entirely because I referred this pressure, uncomfortable, annoying, hateful, to my instinctive being rather than complaining, blaming, pressing back – is that my instinct shapes this pressure for me. It does that right before my eyes, out in the open, where I can lay a finger on it. I write an essay. I pick up a book and read it. I cook a meal for someone. I practice a musical instrument. I figure out the tax returns for old Mrs. Sloane. I sort stuff out in the garden. I buy a ticket for the Carlingford Ferry. I show a few youngsters how to skip rope.

The point being here, that this does me good and I know it. I have become empowered due to the pressure the world exerted on me and on account of my referral of it to my faculty of human instinct. I enjoy the power because it is good power. It does not help me to lord it over anyone but it helps me do good, which is just plain enjoyable.

Of course all this doing I have mentioned, which was done creatively because based on human instinct, can also be done badly, if not based on my human instinct, in which case there is nothing in it for me.

The modern mind-set distinguishes between selfish and generous, between self-centred and magnanimous, but this presupposes that there really is a way for me to decide what is good for someone by judging according to his or her attributes, while whatever good I do to suit myself seems to lie under suspicion of selfishness.

Meanwhile let us not forget that the benefit of religion is indisputable. We do well to recognize the need, within us, to distance ourselves from influences that endlessly externalize us and would persuade us to learn a multitude of skills and to perform a multitude of tasks that would allow us to survive externally, in the absence of the specific wisdom that can only be acquired by heeding its origin within us as we learn to live in accordance with such wisdom. I have described in detail elsewhere how modernity is in fact an unwillingness to recognize that our various afflictions and griefs are positive signs that we are liberated beings, so that modern man characteristically strives not only to ignore these signs and to obliterate them as much as possible rather than heeding them creatively, but it is also, of course, every possible attempt to find satisfaction and happiness externally in a finite, law-ridden world. The impulse to search for an inward basis for ourselves before we impress and express ourselves outwardly can usefully, even nowadays, be described as religious, inasmuch as a spirit other and greater than the spirit of man is taken into consideration during the essential search for our fundamental inward being. Perhaps it still needs to be added that for this search to be successful, this spirit must be merciful good spirit of love.

Modern man, as such, is of course a mythic reality, however a reality all the same. Who can point to himself even nowadays and say with hand on heart that he is entirely free at all times of that existential anxiety! We do well indeed and are exceptionally fortunate if we are not merely blinded to that anxiety due to our hectic activity and frantic business but we recognize it for what it is and know how to overcome it creatively.

To that end then we acquaint ourselves with the cosmic implications of our human-instinctive creativity. We recognize the anxiety where- and whenever it arises, always as the timely reminder that it is of our present need for general repentance and for searching within ourselves for the human-instinctive advantage and good that is ours for enjoyment and use.

First of all we want to be inwardly at home, there can be no doubt about that. Then, in order to continue to have a home within ourselves and among the members of our community, we set examples, by our doing and behaving.

The human instinct I mean, which is like a rock on which we may build within ourselves, serves as the foundation and mainspring of our cosmic significance. Now and again we meet a person who is especially endowed with that rock-like instinct for world community and we feel it in our bones that yes, such is the quality of character and range of personality on which the life of truth and beauty may rest supreme. We do not necessarily seek the company of that person, though we may, but we are put in mind of a general human giftedness that must be available within ourselves as well; and so it is. The discovery of it within ourselves may tax our individuality to the utmost.

Repentance, like humility, like meekness and mildness: those are all instinctive and they vouch for our success as we search for what it takes to build world community. Not by insisting on pride of place but by ceding priority do we arrive at our goal.

*

We should also make an effort to understand faith as instinctive.

We cannot refer some influence on us of the world to our instinct human natural being unless we do so in faith. How could it be otherwise? Of course it makes no sense to call this a religious faith because it certainly exists prior to any distance that has crept in between us and good spirit. It is just plain human natural faith and we are born with it. What has happened to it in the meanwhile, under the influence of State, Religion,

38

Society etc. is anybody's guess. Once thought- and feeling-systems are forced upon us, we may suppose we must 'believe in them' and this is a kind of artificial or "little" faith that does not reach into our elemental being whence all that is truthful and certain is derived. We who have faith do not have a faith, or a Faith. (I capitalize to show respect.) Our faith is instinct, not extinct. It is not derived from credential definition but it stimulates our willingness to be human towards other beings.

So we may have to rediscover our faith, if it has been over-laid by quantities of world influence that has become ingrained in us rather than having been contemplated by us instinctively. It makes good sense to call such unreferred world influence dead matter. We can only sustain a certain amount of dead matter before we die under it. The dead walk around in our vicinity and are burdened by so much dead matter that sometimes our hearts go out to them and we would like to see them rescued from their godless state. Meanwhile we exercise our faith whenever we accept some burden for the purpose of good work, as we are prompted creatively from within ourselves or from within our community.

*

Because the impulse, the prompt, for world community – not for world society or world empire – comes from within ourselves and also from within our community, we might be smart to take another look at what we mean by community, because we certainly do not mean all those who think like we do or who have the same ideal, idol or hero. Also community does not mean society, and while those who work towards a tolerant society of fair-minded people earn our respect, a social goal can never encompass more than a limited ethnic group, no matter how thoroughly the marvellous differences between races are eroded by precisely such social or socialist ambitions. Personally I would steer away from even the expression 'within a society' or 'within society', precisely because instinctive promptings to achieve world community are never social.

Even if, by society, we mean that laudatory approach to community to which we referred earlier – that exploratory effort to extend our community if possible – we certainly have no such thing as a society in mind; whenever promptings to community or even to world community arise in fully-fledged members of society, these have to be falsified or even rejected and denied. As a consequence, individuality, that precious commodity, is distorted and crippled. Enter the sociologist and the sociopathologist, who aim to teach such people how to cope without a soul.

Soul encompasses individuality and community. Those are communal beings who value their inward promptings to community. So here we arrive at yet another definition of communality, namely as our willingness to share our differences creatively with others. A lack of readiness to do so turns us into individuals instead of persons. An outright refusal to do so condemns us to lead the life of individualists and our only hope for togetherness is the impersonal crowd.

The most hopeful definition of social behaviour would have it as experiment towards the possibility of personal community. Community then, if the experiment pans out, implies a successful sharing of individual differences, such as during personal communication. Not a lot of brain is required for understanding that even for the experiment to succeed, unconditional love is required. If we close any doors to start with, such as when we say that we cannot bear selfish people, we will end in a society and cut our losses. Human natural affection, by definition absent in modern society, has a chance again, once we show ourselves capable of sustaining personal community and real friendship.

*

While a society by definition is closed to those with a different identity, a community is potentially open to all. My community extends as far as those with whom I choose to communicate and readily includes those who wish to communicate with me. It cannot be identified because it simply springs from personal good will and from a readiness for creative work.

We know now that creative work overcomes, coincidentally, hindrances to community. The difference between creative work and so-called 'good works' is perhaps more understandable now. If I help an elderly lady across the street, this is readily classed as a good, moral work. What if she didn't want my help and secretly thought of me as an interfering nuisance? What if I just wanted her away from my shop where she so often annoys my customers? All that and much more, infinitely more, does not have to be considered if my helping her stemmed from a creative impulse involving compassion and a readiness to desist if she did not want to be helped. I suppose we might take it for granted that if we have our eye on the merit, we are bound to lose out, one way or another. People sometimes laud someone as a hero because he did what anyone would have done had he been similarly prompted. There is nothing heroic about acting on communal instinct.

What I describe as community, even as your or my community, is in essence world community. Before I act, I do not first ask whether my action might be raised to the level of general validity for all. I merely make sure that it stems from a human-instinctive impulse. After a time, more and more of our thoughts, feelings, doing and behaviour will originate instinctively, in response to some impression of the world or innately.

*

All too rarely it happens that someone has what it takes to support impressions not only from world environment that im-

41

pinge upon his nature but also more directly from his human nature, in which case he is capable of teaching and guidance. Such a one then hearkens upon the promptings of good spirit. He may call good spirit father and the one sent by the father brother and friend. A little should be said about this relationship.

Divine and human nature as one reside in such a one. Since he is truly human he is at once mortal and immortal. To put it colloquially, if he is not careful he is liable to die and if he plays his cards right he has eternal life and does not die. The present work however is for all whose being impinges upon *world environment.* That is the environment that will eventually house the human community. All in that community either do not die, or if they die they live again.

*

World environment impinges upon us and addresses us in a great variety of ways, and all these ways are mysterious. We read them off our own human nature, clearly so to the extent of our apperceptive equipment.

Surely it helps us to be certain that our world environment is such that we are to thrive. We do not exist for the world but our world for us. With that in mind we may have to question our attitude on a daily basis, especially inasmuch as we suppose it might be up to us to change that environment. Really what may be required is that we stop interfering. Also we need to differentiate between earth and world. The earth is our garden and we are responsible for its maintenance. Nothing better than insight into world community to inform us of how best to maintain the earth and to benefit from its great diversity of goods. As a matter of fact world-community knowledge and understanding of earth-maintenance go hand in hand. As we advance in the one we improve in the other.

*

42

World-community thinking is a different story from global thinking. We really are not part of the globe, are we. It floats there beneath us, glorious, impressive, unrelated. We see it from outer space and outer space thinking is more like an intellectualist game than a serious consideration of a human/divine life-support system that empowers us in line with our most genuine, constructive desires.

Globally we alight, comment and flit off. How thrilling to be able to imagine the whole thing – as a thing, because as a thing it is obviously in our superior hands. Those who speak of global concerns often sound to me like upper class parents visiting the children once a month and leaving instructions with the Nanny. Global consciousness is what produces international panaceas and common denominators. When something 'goes viral', usually on the internet these days, it could also be described as 'going global'. It's everywhere. Everybody knows, has heard – and forgets as quickly.

Besides I don't like to think of myself as standing on a globe. My experience of the earth will always be of a generally flat terrain. How marvellous, that when you walk far enough you are liable to end up where you started! That sums up so much for me. I become suspicious of those who are not dizzied by the notion of interplanetary travel. Do they really reside on the earth to start with? If not, I take pains to avoid them. The house I live in, where my wife and I raised our children and challenged each other to become more human, is a home now so rich in memory of achievement and in achievement of life support that now and again we laugh at the absurdity of ever choosing to move elsewhere.

No, people who cannot wait to circle the globe have never really lived on the earth; I call that one of my dearest prejudices.

I have another: Have they ever experienced world as it was in the beginning and ever shall be for those who grow and change and create rather than forever getting tied up in world- and society-improvement? Have they ever known world without end, stripped of all that mythic clobber that is meant to make us feel great while in truth it diminishes our status beneath that of the bee hive and the ant colony?

World community certainly implies world without end, without popular fail-safe measures and self-destroy functions. It implies world influence that is mysterious and sacramental: not mysterious inasmuch as it cannot be explained, which is a wrong notion of *mystery* but rather in that *it supplies us with energy innately and directly*. Not only that but the energy is pure and dream-like, like sunshine to trees as they rise to it and absorb it in their needles and leaves. Why are we also endowed with this thirst for growth and increase, if not in order to rise joyfully and instinctively to every occasion of this mysterious impression on us, this sacramental encouragement to think of ourselves as at once perfect, powerful and benign?

*

As for the origin of life, what a tragic misnomer! What modern man calls life is at best survival.

Things appear, stay around for a while, then disappear. However things, as we know, are not beings, which we behold. While we are modern, we behold nothing. We sense data and things are collections of data, of indiscriminate bits into which things dissolve at a moment's notice. Soon we get bored with these things and look for other ones – or we buy a new one, after we've dumped the old one. Those were things too.

In reality there are only beings, not things. As soon as we approach beings in a shabby way, with an indistinct imagination for example, they are bound to hide from us behind a film of thingness. The thinness of thingness is impenetrable except to our human natural instinctive apparatus. That is how we improve. We rescue beings from the thingness we ourselves have caused or allowed to happen. The resurrection of things, let's face it, implies our own resurrection.

So what is the beginning or origin of life? Silly question. Life itself is the beginning. It is the beginning of all that is and has being.

Once we understand life correctly as the beginning, we may then behold the behaviour of beings as life-giving, enlivening, vitalizing and the like.

This may seem like a revolutionary change from the modern attitude, which looks at (listens to, feels for, etc.) appearances and catalogues their alterations and then comes up with legal references for those alterations. This takes a lot of time, centuries, progress is slow, we tire ourselves out and just before we give up we notice something that surpasses our diminishing expectations. The truth, after all, is just around the corner. Shall we call it intelligent design, this time round? Why not. Mr. Darwin was close; we have finally stumbled on the answer. In school our six-year-olds were taught that 'God made the world', which perhaps meant very little to them, but mostly on account of the way it was put to them it got them started on a life of mistrusting their individual and authentic thought. Perhaps we have rediscovered God under our powerful microscopes – as a thing? God may just be the very first appearance after all – or no, not an appearance but a hypothesis that sets off sequences of appearances. After that we have causality, we have chance and beyond that the wind blows. Why get angry.

*

World impresses mysteriously and influences sacramentally all that is.

Beings are alive and live. In the beginning there was life. Whatever begins today is lively. Whatever decides to begin tomorrow will live. How do we know? Because life is the beginning, as we may notice all around us. Beings testify to that beginning and we wrong ourselves by approaching them as though they were things – turning into things ourselves as a consequence while we debate our impoverishment.

So in our misguided search for the origin of life we clearly have to begin with something that is dead – which for some reason, which has escaped us so far, is suddenly alive. What has happened in the meanwhile? That is what we want to find out. The definition of dead? Well, matter, I suppose. Surely matter is dead. Just to make sure, let us call it mere matter or dead matter. You have to start somewhere. It should suffice that we turn our imagination off while we look at matter and then turn it on again when cells start to multiply. Our intelligence then prompts us: Why should matter be dead? What is matter in any case, when it eats and breeds on the earth: rock salt? Iron ore?

Things lead to things and to more things. They breed like rabbits. Every seven years mixematosis wipes them out and we are reminded: That is all they are, just things. Treat them like beings and they stay healthy.

*

Beings are not things. Nor is world the world. *World influences us*. We forever try to influence the world. We have to try to stop doing that if world influence is ever to reveal itself to us as the healing, sane and empowering influence that it is. Could this be made plainer?

We want to influence the world in order to have things our own way. Who in their right mind would try to have things in the first place? Then of course we want them our own way to confirm ourselves all the better as things: individuals and individualists rather than persons with character and creative individuality.

A candidate for the American presidency "sets forth a doctrine for the exercise of American influence in the world." And again: "David Cameron needs to extend Britain's influence in the world." What is all this foolishness? Are these not archaic principles trotted out by populists to excite those who are beginning to suspect that really and truly there is nothing of value or quality to be gained in that direction but they have not yet a clue as to an alternative?

The pseudo-thinking is of course that of the gang: Unless we hit them first, they will hit us. Those who have achieved a way of life that deserves the name set a good example. Others may imitate. For gang members, whether on the street or internationally, force is always a more or less concealed item on the agenda.

The end or goal of the world is to survive, at any cost – and to fail. Whether it fails with a bang or a whimper is surely beside the point. The big bang theory of the beginning of the universe (the universe has never begun, nor will it ever end, for heaven's sake!) is really a blinkered attempt to ban the fear of a big-bang-end-of-the-world into history – and not only into history, but so far back in time we may as well forget about it.

World too is without end. In the end both the universe and the world pass away, for each and all of us, so the question is: Do we have world and universe without end to fall back on? Not that we need to wait until we fall. We can climb out right now by ushering in world and universe influence – ushering it in, welcoming it, rather than forever rolling boulders in its way, the boulders of our misguided attempts to influence and rule the world and to wonder about the origin of life and the universe.

47

World- and universe-influence, in turn, are one and the same life-giving and life-supportive blessing. What a change!

*

World, that would influence us beneficially, we turn into a thing by trying to influence it.

If, who knows for how long, we have continued to influence and change this thing, now and again realizing that *plus ça change, plus c'est la même chose*, then obviously no quick philological reminder is going to persuade us of the truth. 'What is he on about, anyway?' we will wonder. No, unless the truth falls in our lap and we tread the path of genius, it will take a shock of sorts to sort us out – if being sorted out is on the cards for us; then years of dedication will flow from that and perhaps a seemingly endless series of wonderful revelations.

On the other hand, millions of people are on the edge – not of the cliff, but of changing their mind about which way the wind blows. A lot of those who are members of one religion or another will make that tiny adjustment in their attitude and suddenly fresh air and light will enter their little room and the door will open – and here they hadn't a notion they were trapped in a confinement of their own making. Cheerfully they repent and discover the community within and among them and when they reach for its limits, behold, world is their community.

World is not a man-made thing like other things – which are all man-made – but created being. World is created being. We are created beings. Is it any wonder we feel at home?

Some become attached to ways of speaking. The addiction to words, to particular definitions of things, plagues the earth's population. Wars have been fought over abstractions. Hair-splitting shortens the lifespan and causes deterioration of the liver. If a particular phrase centres our faculties for a day or

48

two, does that mean the entire neighbourhood should genuflect before it? I for my part find that the advice and the injunctions of Jesus do wonders for me, but only if I live them. I hope and pray it will never again occur to me to argue about them. Once you have got hold of what turns the pages of the book of life for you, use it, work it, show the results. As for your recipe, wait till you're asked. Plenty of time then to unwrap a few secrets, once you know who is talking to you. If you're a preacher, for god's sake choose your words carefully, and let them be your own words, not repetitions of what you've read, wherever you've read it. Consider carefully, the very sound of your voice is liable to drive people to drink.

*

The morality, not the ethic yet, of world community is simply religious. Behave the way you want to be treated and overcome your dirty emotions. Ask for help if you cannot manage it yourself. Keep in mind that in yourself you are human natural, which implies a perfectly suitable way of life, and take note of how easy it is to lose track of what is important in this department. When you have lost track, make it your priority to find your way back. If you don't know how to love, make that your priority. You may have to start with good will, but don't stop there. Remember that religion has nothing to do with any particular Religion (respect!). The most effective and mutually satisfying morality steers clear of particular Religions, which have mostly turned into social affairs, into observance and ceremonial. World community cannot spring from a Religion, especially not from those who insist they are the true, one and only orthodox article and if you do not join you may as well bury your head in shame because the law of God will find you out and you will be rejected from the final reward, whatever that is.

Remember that your god is the god of the living, not of the dead. (Mk.12:27)

A short definition of moral world-community is all the people you love and that includes your enemies. If you hate your enemy, your morality is sterile and your community gets locked in. Protestants who hate Catholics and Catholics who hate Protestants know nothing of world community and their morality stinks. As members of Religions we have to gear down our love to tolerance, a poor substitute because not communal. Also, when we limit our community to those we like, our individuality falls asleep. We are not created to like but to love.

As soon as we reach out to the disadvantaged we become ethical in our outlook because we want to do good and because we appreciate the empowering aspect of doing good. However doing good is sometimes not the easiest thing in the world be-cause we tend to get light-headed and decent intentions turn into indecent interference. The old adage holds, that a moral base has to support an ethical structure. In the absence of un-conditional love we come up with an ethical stance at best. This is why so many good intentions fail, because we do not first take ourselves in hand, settle our emotions and passions and ask ourselves what we really have in mind here other than material expansion.

Just as morality in the absence of true religion becomes hypocritical, so does ethics, if we do not do real good, become vain. Only unconditional love can prevent vanity. We may suppose our intention is good but we are only bolstering our ego. In unconditional love god is involved, whether we like it or not. How absurd that we should ever need to pretend that the creature exists in the absence of the creator! We know both men and god by their works and an ethical person is the most noble work of god.

50

So by loving the one we intend to help, we also love god, it goes without saying. And dare we ask, is any love that does not involve god really worth it? However we must distinguish the god who loves human beings whether they love him or not, from the One who needs to be bribed and appeased and who places burdens on people, the bearing of which does them no good.

*

All that is able to influence us truly we call god and world. There is the love from within and the love from without. Some benefit from the one only and some from both.

World-influence is proverbial and symbolic. This is how mystery sways us towards life. We are at liberty to close ourselves off in a myriad ways, all of which involve making of world a thing, calling it the world and then becoming involved by and attached to that thing – while god weeps. Hence the saying: If we love the world we do not love god.

World without end is a concept weighted positively and in the direction opposite to the world, which is a thing. The end of that thing is everywhere misunderstood because it is merely to remind us that this thing too has neither value nor use.

By withdrawing from the world, from this ineffectual thing we call the world, we do not automatically benefit from the love that is god, proverbially and symbolically, mysteriously and sacramentally. World cannot influence us until we are fully regenerated morally and religiously. Humility, meekness and mildness are of the essence. Through practice of these we manage both, a coincidental turning from the world of things and the moral renewal that makes us accessible to world influence that is indirect love of god. God is merciful good spirit of love.

*

This brings us to *god* that is directly *love from within*, specifically *merciful love*. It suffices that we are merciful to those around us for this direct good influence to teach us and guide us in every way. There is a difference between forgiving and being merciful. The latter, as the word shows, is a way of being, whereas we forgive instead of holding something against someone in the sense of criticism, hatred, vengefulness and the like. By forgiving we save ourselves the troubles and problems incurred through blaming and condemning. By being merciful and therefore showing mercy we make ourselves accessible to merciful good spirit. The result is the blessedness for which all hanker who seek happiness and good fortune or luck.

*

Now there is something we see the world over, endemic in every small or large population, due to which merciful human being, as our own authentic inheritance, rarely sees the light of day, and on those occasions when it does, we find it ill recognized, poorly understood and all too soon discouraged and blighted.

Let us first try to come to grips with the fact that merciful being is not a particular state of human being but human being itself. *Human being is merciful.* So to the extent that we have become divorced from our human being and become less than human beings, we may achieve repair by choosing to be merciful. That much is in our hands.

A shortfall in human natural being does not necessarily present as merciless behaviour, especially if we equate mercy with nothing more than judicial forgiving or clemency. What should alert us to this deplorable condition is that we are out of order, even disorderly. We behave in ways that in anyone else would seem to us embarrassing and even shameful. We demonstrate arrogance and unwarranted antagonism, when that is not what we expect of ourselves. However mostly, and most

52

seriously, we indulge in thinking and feeling of a type, in sentiments and opinions, that certainly we would judge as unworthy of a human being – if we were reflectively inclined.

This *reflective inclination*, which could also be described as a readiness to see ourselves as we are at any given time, needs to be nourished and cherished or it leaves us in the lurch.

Because we learn and grow in maturity, this reflective inclination must time and again be recognized by us – and recognitions is the salient point here. We cannot make a habit of reflective inclination – of seeing ourselves as we are, because circumstances and the demands made on us cause us forever to need to adapt, to invent and to challenge, and in all those cases, as in many more that are growth- and change-related, our inclination to reflect on who we are cannot but be interrupted and disturbed.

However we may at any time recognize, and even *tend to recognize*, that something is amiss and only a little practice will then cause us to be reminded that what is amiss is a lack of reflection on how we are – which leads directly to the choice to be merciful and therefore to be fully fledged human natural beings again.

We *tend* to recognize that something is amiss. That much is given us. We *incline* to reflect on how we are. That too is a gift. Whenever the inclination leaves us, the tendency takes over. The one action that depends on us is the decision to be merciful again. And remember, mercy is not clemency or simple forgiveness, though these surely spring from it. Little children are merciful. This cannot be observed too often. Those who make the wellbeing and upbringing of little children their concern will make the most fortunate connection with them through merciful being.

Although the reflective inclination cannot become habitual and spontaneous for us – and only those who cease from learning, developing and evolving will suppose they succeed in this, while in fact they merely turn critical – we can nevertheless nourish and cherish it while we have the benefit of it, and we do this by way and means of any creative activity that becomes possible for us, such as caring conversation, cheerful home-making, a helpful invention, the writing of a worthwhile book or the judicious cultivation of a kitchen garden. Joy will automatically play a role if we take it easy.

*

Now that we have acquainted ourselves a little with merciful human natural being, especially inasmuch as we now realize how we default and may recuperate, we intend to have a look at what it is that so casually, the world over, causes not only individuals but entire populations not only to steer clear of merciful behaviour but to ignore it altogether, although without it their human nature must always remain deplorably in question.

Instinctively, innately, we know ourselves as human natural beings and therefore as merciful. Consequently we feel disoriented and adversely judged when we behave, or are, otherwise. How does this happen? How can we get back to how we were and want to be?

Surely the combination of the reflection to which we incline and the recognition to which we tend should do the trick. By taking advantage of those two gifts or blessings we are bound to find our way back, even though it may take a while. If the inclination to reflect has escaped us, surely we will recognize what is amiss and choose to be merciful.

Quite possible that out there,
as sunlight and air,
radio waves mimic
an absolutely different gimmick.

As the elements draw nigh,
it occurs to us by and by
to service our receiver sets
for otherworldly internets.

The idea is to keep still,
using intellect or will,
it matters little which,
to make that all-important switch

from magic, tentative intent,
to mystery and sacrament.
You may not know the rules yet
but they're not hard to get.

Merely put yourself out,
let world have its clout.
I don't mean the world, that thing
that forever looks for its king.

At one time it was called
the logos – then it stalled
and took a tragic turn;
modernity – drown or burn.

Perhaps you can hear it hiss
as it gobbles that and this,
that great garden snake,
ever so busy for our sake.

*

    The most frequent mistake and error that causes the world-wide mayhem to which I have alluded is the misunderstanding of the two gifts I have mentioned. We misconceive the reflective inclination, which is a gift or blessing and abuse it as though it were an instrument or tool, which we might with equanimity take up or lay aside and with which we might operate more or less cleverly, honestly, astutely etc.

And, of course, to the extent that we do not accept the reflective inclination as a gift, we have nothing else then that will clarify for us our disorientation and disorder, so we merrily congratulate ourselves as we proceed along the tragically modern path of destruction, which has, but for exceptions, been the way of the world for two millennia. Always there have been some who recognized which way the wind blew. We might say that they had the wits, as such exceptions to the popular run of the mill have today, to know world without end as the original creation that it is and to say what they knew, as best they knew, under prevailing circumstances.

As human beings we know ourselves as gifted and this should go without saying but it does not. We have what is good as a gift, we ignore the gift and strive and struggle to earn and achieve what is nearly good. We want credit for that. Admiration. Money. Those who are merciful and know it show us mercy. They know why they are merciful, namely to allow them to approach us in our misery with forbearance and love.

How quick are we not to say to someone in misery, in trouble, someone complaining of the pain of misfortune: It serves you right, for being so stupid, so aggressive, so lazy, so different from me. No wonder you are having a hard time, considering your false religion, your bad morals and temper, your wrong political persuasion. At best we withdraw into our superior self, practice non-interference. What are we supposed to do?

This may be an honest question. What should we do instead, other than prevent ourselves from getting sucked into the same misery? When we see those who kick a man when he's down we count ourselves virtuous by comparison.

56

The merciful man would argue: First of all, my merciful attitude actually does prevent me from getting 'sucked into' someone's misery because of the inherent compassion implied by merciful love. Then, when I see someone heading off down a dangerous road, it occurs to me how best to warn him because I observe him mercifully. The path he takes may in point of fact appear dangerous to me while being quite safe for him, in which case it will occur to me to mind my own business. Finally, although for a moment selfishness may surface in me, I will quickly recognize this as a disorder and incline to reflect, then choosing merciful being over selfishness, which act is one of the most creative and ethically powerful acts of which I, as a human being, am capable.

*

The troubled modern individual, divided in himself, does sense the pain of this: the mental conflict and the spiritual uncertainty. He cannot recognize what ails him because what does ail him is his sacrificial philosophy of life, due to his lack of merciful being. He cannot recognize what is wrong because he abuses the gift of reflective inclination which gift must, in practice and use, precede his use of the other half of what one might call this salvific benefit, of which all human beings are privileged to partake, namely the tendency to recognize what, in truth, we miss, namely merciful being.

If we abuse the first half – and I specifically speak of two halves because I wish to accommodate our modern self-division – the second half is not available to us. We understand well enough that we cannot make a habit of reflective inclination, though we do well to practice it. However losing touch with it is not at all the same as actually abusing it. If we use the gift as though it were our right, the giver withdraws, can no longer appear to us except as a thing, and we are left with a myth and no longer a reality.

Also, reflective inclination is not a thing. In other words, right of ownership under the law is not relevant. Call it instead a mode of being. What we have learned of the difference between beings and things should help us here. (Note what some Christians have made of the being Christ calls the true bread, himself, the 'coming bread', by blithely referring to it as 'our daily bread', in the prayer they like to repeat and repeat, which was given them as a model: Pray like this! and they have made a thing itself out of this too.)

*

More needs to be said about this tragic modern misappropriation and malpractice of reflective inclination.

How do we normally take account of a spiritual gift in the first place? We are moved to feel, think, behave etc. in terms and in line with it. All spiritual gifts put us in touch with the spirit that (or who) is the giver. That spirit, we might say, is somewhat within some part of us. If we mean good spirit, we need not any further specify. The donor of the reflective inclination we mean here is merciful good spirit, or simply good spirit, or god, as I usually spell the word, in comparison to the God that has been set up as a thing. (One has to make one's point somehow.)

So when we are moved by good spirit to reflect on our human natural being, is that guaranteed to please us right away? Well, it depends on how thoroughly we are wrapped up in ourselves at the time. At one extreme, if I have never before considered the possibility of merciful being and have only ever reflected as an act of will or intellect on a thing, who knows what thing or things, then I may be in trouble for a time, in a way that depends entirely on my emotional make-up. If it happens several times, I may come up with a reason for it, which I arrive at by reflecting on my troubled condition in a fearful way, which process is well known, by those who know mercy,

58

to produce myths. I will think in the following or a similar manner: My confusion is obviously caused by an agent. I will find a name for this agent and will try to influence it/him/her in a way to persuade him to leave me alone.

You notice that I do this by reflecting. It happens to be the very form good spirit used to address me, and now I use it to deliver a fearful message of supplication, pleading, bribing. In fact I am willing to harm my own self, albeit in a controlled fashion and on my own terms, so as to get ahead of the gift of reflective inclination, which is unexpected, confusing, troubling – you name it.

In short, I have opted for sacrifice instead of mercy. Any future attempt by merciful spirit to get through to me may well have no better effect than to cause me to differentiate my superstitions to the point where I get together with others and eventually we agree on a whole collection of sacrificial acts, which will harden into a system of legislative and putatively religious observancies. Meanwhile merciful good spirit does not give up on us and eventually all hell breaks loose for those who insist on their forbidding reaction even in the face of this spirit's appearance in person one earth. He too has to be sacrificed, for the sake of peace and quiet and political expediency and security. Meanwhile those who have long given up on sacrifice have the benefit of his teachings and of his presence within and among them. The plurality still continue to 'worship' the sacrifice. Those who love merciful good spirit have nothing to do with sacrifice and worship mercifully in reality and in the truth.

*

Merciful, human natural being, then, implies an awareness of our being whole. When we come across some who are not whole and suffering on account of that, our heart goes out to them, due to our being merciful, and we may decide to grow, to

59

do ourselves some good by sharing their burden. We are not removed or separate from them by expertise or profession or rank and therefore not prevented from seeing ourselves in the same human condition and liable to similar temptations and misfortunes.

If, during the course of our compassionate communality, we become strained or stressed, we are delighted to find that this is brought to our attention and we renew our commitment to merciful human being. We know that we live eternally, which also implies that if we die we live again. This 'living again' itself implies a gain, for we have grown, perhaps in the power to do good. Those who think of themselves as good and dispense goodness to the less fortunate and to those of a lower worldly standing, really have nothing going for them and we leave them to their superior self-respect.

If we refuse to suffer when we find ourselves disoriented and instead we harden ourselves to the pain and let the supposed misfortune harden our hearts and stiffen our necks, this does not make the present and challenging merciful good spirit go away. If it did, it would not be merciful. This hardening and stiffening process then 'counter-presents', as we might call it, and it does this most commonly by producing pseudo-religious myths. We end up with golden calves, such as the materialistic society; with a plurality of supposed divinities, such as in some eastern populations, with hard and fast rules and laws that began as kindly suggestions and wise precepts and now they oppress the unwary and misdirect the gullible.

How does it come that these superstitions and myths masquerade as holy mysteries and divine sacraments, thus barring access to the real mysteries and sacraments? How do they get away with it for so long? Why are they allowed to persist?

The answer to that must be sought in the psychology of any resistance to merciful good spirit, which is after all, one supposes, a kind of negative recognition of it. Even in the demonic dimension itself we sometimes come across a reflection of this phenomenon, such as when the great Bonaparte does not conceal his admiration for the leader of a Prussian faction he has destroyed, when he says: 'How could you possibly have arrived at the decision to resist me?'

Surely we can see how much more than this our resistance of merciful good spirit is bound to infect us with a negative and ultimately self-destructive, roundly stated: bad spirituality.

*

We have arrived at the crux of the matter that makes world community unlikely. However what is more important is that we have identified what makes it possible.

Once we understand the difference between merciful being and the sacrificial way of life we are bound to choose the former, however the very involvement in and commitment to the sacrificial way of life all but rules out such understanding, so what we are faced with is a hard core of those who espouse merciful being and a peripheral plurality of those who insist on the sacrificial way of life.

The onus is on those who espouse merciful being to engage – not in society, which by itself is not road to anywhere – but in social community, by which I mean social involvement of the purpose to, and to the end of, world community. We are bound to engage socially with strangers until we know whether world-community is possible. If not, we lose nothing. If yes, much is gained.

*

The choice to be merciful is tantamount to the option for human nature and the intention to be a mature human being.

61

We know by now that at this level of rational life-engagement we are not concerned about man or interested in mankind so much as we find ourselves in the presence of men, women and children. We look at what happens from one day to the next and we cope with what happens to the best of our ability. Our works confirm us existentially and create communal bridges. How we act and behave continually joins up with how we think and feel, so that we are engaged in an ongoing process of world community.

Usually and commonly the choice to be merciful can be described more relevantly as a choice to be merciful instead, because while we are merciful we do not give it a second thought. However we increase from without and grow from within and we dare not rest on our laurels. So when suddenly we notice an inclination to reflect, we do well to take this as an invitation and an encouragement, to renegotiate, if you like, our merciful being. What is required here is something like a linking up with a new set of circumstances, like an alignment of ourselves with additional experience, or like a going out of our way to interpret different demands being made on us and translating the result into our own language, which is the language then in which we will offer it to others as digestible goods.

All these describe ways of being merciful *again*. We really should not think of it as other than a time-consuming process. We cannot say ahead of time how long it will take until we are right in our skin and well in flesh and spirit again. What we know meanwhile is that our time is being well spent by us and that we waste none of it.

*

Should any serious question arise as to the need and availability for mercy we might respond in the following manner. Merciful good spirit in person is historic. As a direct result that personality is available to all, primarily by way of their human nature and secondarily by means of world-mystery and world sacrament.

With gratitude and admiration one turns to the culture through which merciful good spirit became personally present among us. With the utmost toleration and respect we view all those who have not opposed the working-out of merciful personality from gifted human nature and do not obstruct the evolution of merciful persons in the light of day.

*

Those who not only do not oppose but actually work on behalf of merciful good spirit, in whatever venue or circle of activity they choose, all help to make it possible that world-community should flourish. Keep in mind this is no ideal state or utopia. It wants to be understood in the light of day among men, women and children on earth, in concrete environments, not in abstract conceptions.

It makes no sense to speak of such work in terms of form and content, however it can be described on the basis of shape.

The worker knows himself to be motivated directly, instinctively, by merciful good spirit, and indirectly, elementally, by impressions (mysterious, sacramental) of world environment.

It can never be a case of just one or the other, however the 'mix' is weighted 'in one direction or the other attraction'. Both direction and attraction always play a role. Inspiration and aspiration are useful terms for the worker, not for the consumer or beneficiary of the work.

*

For the escape-artist from modernity, whose distinguishing mark, however expressed, is always and unavoidably a version of 'let's get out of here!', popularity is what counts, because as he makes a name for himself he survives. We recognize his worth, because, no matter how modestly or magnificently, depending on available funds, he does show the modern tragedy (and comedy) for what it amounts to and is. If he does his job well, he passes no judgment, neither pro nor con, and steers well away from criticism and adulation. That way we learn to see ourselves in our modern two-dimensionality and do not despair of the self-contradiction at our very soul. After one fashion or another we are comforted. Meanwhile we carry on in our two-dimensionality, which leaves us at liberty to stray to port or starboard but steerage is out of our hands.

The escape-artist, of whatever productive persuasion, manages, for the duration of his work, to rise above the modern limitations and afterwards settles back into them, content to continue until the idea or notion for the next work occurs to him. From the eternal point of view his good effect is medical and medicinal, inasmuch as he identifies symptoms and then assuages. The healing of the underlying discrepancy cannot be asked of him as his responsibility. If we then make good use of the postponement, that is entirely up to us. To be pitied are those who fill their cupboards and drawers with medication and never look beyond the desire to survive as long and as painlessly as possible.

In a thoroughly materialistic society, the escape-artist is of paramount importance because of the widespread need for assurance that materialism may be bearable. He flourishes beyond expectation, beyond his wildest hopes at times. Meanwhile he is modern and at fault until he does more than escape for a moment, from the modern predicament. However he would have to be gifted in that direction. Perhaps he is and has not yet noticed.

In that case it would occur to him to diagnose his human condition and he would then actually have to do so and not merely indulge in arrogance or moaning, depending on the side of the ship to which he fled.

*

Not the condition of society or of the world the reflective escape-artist would have to diagnose, *but his own*. Unaccustomed as he might be to such an endeavour and perhaps much habituated to letting the characteristically modern doubts and sentiments escape from him in contradictory fashion, he would yet discipline his attentiveness and master, in a sense, his indulgences and extravagances. Clarity touching on his own, individual condition would allow light to fall on the condition of others. He would extend his familiarity with pain from which we try to escape – to pain which we suffer. He would learn compassion.

He would begin to differentiate between thinking about and thinking, between feeling and feelings, emotion and emotions, perhaps even between things and beings, although before he arrives at that last insight he might well decide to cut his losses and dedicate himself to a sympathetic, if not compassionate, representation of the human condition under modern and perhaps even ancient constraints. In that case he does not remove himself from the modern condition so as to be able to represent it, more or less accurately, but he suffers the condition, more or less gladly and shows how he copes, in terms of pity and fellow feeling. It does not escape him that now he is much more of a human being than when he was merely an escape-artist and this gives him satisfaction. In fact it would be unfair to call him an artist now because he has begun to work creatively, to overcome hindrances in himself to the development of his humanity and to care about whether those around him live or merely exist.

We who avail ourselves of the fruits of his labours may well decide to follow his example. He shows us that something

65

good may be possible that had not occurred to us and that something may be desirable which until now we had shunned.

*

We know them by their works.

We look at the escape-artist's productions and decide whether he gives in to the inclination to reflect on his inward being and, in other words, receives and invests that gift, or else insists on his modern popularity at any cost, mostly at the cost of his soul, by expropriating the gift and producing – not creating – the "great wonders" that bring the populace to its knees, in adulation – as they lose their heads under the influence of demonic agencies and attractions.

We do well to acquaint ourselves to some degree with the difference between demonic productions and creative works. The latter, as we mentioned above, exemplify the importance of compassion and suffering, while the former are not really exemplary at all but simply monstrous. What is so sad is the readiness, always, of a large section of every population to be beguiled by what is nothing but big, not to mention huge, gigantic and the like. Instead of choosing inward reflection, one is taken in by outside spectacles and prodigies, which, on account of their size, albeit mere size, seem to promise total protection against the fear and terror initially set off by any implied need to look at oneself and think about what one sees. Finally anything monstrous should make us think rather than causing us to abandon thought altogether. If we use tools, this can be done reflectively. The demonic impulse dispenses with reflection and seems to insist – drawing us in if we are not careful – on monstrous behaviour. If that does not make us think, we are truly lost and in need of external reminder, which can be defined as catastrophic.

Creative works arise due to the reflective inclination that informs us of our human natural giftedness with humanity and life, but also of any reluctance on our part to live as mature human beings. This may not sound like a tall order but all too often it is. Why should we be reluctant to live? Because we have become addicted to survival. Why should we shun human being? Because we are too arrogant to repent.

Any creative work worth its salt introduces us, in one way or another, to life and human being. We become convinced of the need to search for the life that is worth living because it does not end in death and we are persuaded, by whatever means and probably without knowing how, that the path to that life leads through the cheerfullest self-abnegation plus sorrow for dysfunction.

*

So an artist refuses to recognize the inclination to reflect on his inward being as a gift and instead expropriates it for his own purpose of escaping, for the duration of his production, from modernity, so as to be able to view it critically, then representing it, filtered through his individuality. The effect he aims at is to comfort and please his public in their modern state. After all he needs to survive, so he must pander to public taste and preference. He has no interest in advancing from modernity to communality. Indeed any such urge that should surface to his consciousness he suppresses 'monstrously' and presents it as spectacle.

Criticism, as the modern disease, is not the same as healthy critique and leads nowhere. It merely channels our dissatisfaction with ourselves into the external world which we help to fashion thereby and where we are never done finding fault and opportunity for change and improvement. So too with the critical escape artist, who has to make his offering interesting, exciting and morally self-indulgent.

67

Meanwhile those who sincerely look for a cure for their modernity do well to stay away from the plentifully available productions of the escape-artist. Anodynes do not cure, but they buy us time. We can also become stupid and addicted to them. It is when the escape-artist becomes demonic and produces monstrosities that he does actual harm because he qualifies and differentiates modernity. He leads thousands to their death in Russia in the name of 'la gloire' perhaps, and kills millions to 'purify' one race of another. Communism, capitalism – what are they except systems devised by modern man to perpetuate himself a little longer – while to the one who senses within himself the true instinct for world-community, all these aberrations, stemming from the deplorable unwillingness to search for the truth, the light, etc. within, are but reminders to continue with his search.

*

The art-worker has found within himself the true source of value and substance and goes on to incorporate – within himself and his works – the world impressions and influences we have defined as mysterious and sacramental. World is no longer a thing for him, to which thing he refers as the world, but he knows and understands it instinctively, faithfully and reasonably. His own growth and the growth of his works amount to the same creative process and organic operation. It makes no sense to think of his works and their effect as cultural. Whether modest or grand, they stand alone and have to be accepted at face value or rejected.

* * *

Subject Index

* * * *